The
WORST-CASE SCENARIO
POCKET GUIDE
CARS

By David Borgenicht &
Ben H. Winters

Illustrations by Brenda Brown

CHRONICLE BOOKS
SAN FRANCISCO

Copyright © 2009 by Quirk Productions, Inc.

Worst-Case Scenario® and The Worst-Case Scenario
Survival Handbook™ are trademarks of Quirk
Productions, Inc.

Library of Congress Cataloging in Publication Data
available.

ISBN: 978-0-8118-7046-7

Manufactured in China
Designed by Jenny Kraemer
Illustrations by Brenda Brown
Visit www.worstcasescenarios.com

10 9 8 7 6 5 4 3 2 1

Chronicle Books LLC
680 Second Street
San Francisco, CA 94107
www.chroniclebooks.com

WARNING: You really should have been more careful. Now you're
facing one of the worst-case scenarios presented in this book—at least
you have the book with you, to refer to. But you must use your good
judgment and common sense and consult a professionally trained
expert to deal with these dangerous situations. The authors, publisher,
and experts disclaim any liability from any injury that may result
from the use, proper or improper, from the information contained
in this book. Nothing herein should be construed or interpreted to
infringe on the rights of other persons or to violate criminal statutes.
We urge you to be respectful and safe.

CONTENTS

INTRODUCTION

There's just something about the open road: the wind in your hair, the radio pumping, the sheer unalloyed terror of realizing you're sitting behind the wheel of a giant, steel death machine, hurtling down the highway with nothing but your own split-second reflexes, the questionable abilities of your fellow drivers, and your car's out-of-warranty safety systems standing between you and your own doom.

Let's not kid around here: cars really ought to be called worst-case scenarios on wheels. From the sweating panic of that very first driver's test, cars and the scary situations they inspire are a staple of modern life. When you're not dealing with an engine that's caught fire, you're facing a sudden brake failure, or driving down a flight of stairs to get away from the guy who's chasing you.

Whether it's driving in hurricane or white-out conditions, bailing out at high speeds, escaping from the trunk of a car, or steering a big rig over the ice roads, you just never know what's coming at you around the next turn. Lucky for you, every one of those situations is covered in this little book, and plenty more besides. So next time you get behind the wheel, make sure you've got *The Worst-Case Scenario Pocket Guide: Cars* (right along with the 23 other items never to leave home without, listed on page 16). It might just save your life—or at least keep you from peeing in your pants before the next rest stop (page 21). Either way, we hope you enjoy the ride.

—The Authors

*You never really learn to swear
until you learn to drive.*
—Anonymous

ROADBLOCKS

HOW TO SURVIVE BEING STRANDED IN THE SNOW

1 **Get as far off the road as possible.**
Drive or push your vehicle fully clear of the roadway, but be sure that your car is still visible to any vehicles that may pass by and be able to offer assistance.

2 **Make your car visible to potential rescuers.**
Turn on your emergency flashers. When the snow stops falling, raise the car's hood to signal distress; when snow begins to fall again, close the hood. Set up flares along the roadside between your car and the road. Hang a brightly colored cloth such as a red scarf or a torn-off piece of blanket from the antenna.

3 | **Spell out HELP in the snow.**
Use rocks and sticks to spell the word HELP in six-foot-long block letters next to the car so your position is visible from the air.

4 | **Stay near the car.**
Do not leave the vicinity of your vehicle unless help is visible within 100 yards. Blowing and drifting snow can be extremely disorienting, causing you to wander away from your car deeper into the snow and become lost. Shelter is your most important priority in inclement weather.

5 | **Put on all available clothing.**
If traveling with clothes, put them on in layers. Wrap yourself in blankets stored in the trunk. Strip the leather or vinyl from your seats and wrap yourself in them.

Spell out "HELP" in the snow with rocks and sticks.

6 | **Run the engine for 10 minutes once an hour.**
Clear snow from the exhaust pipe and crack one upwind window to keep carbon monoxide from building up in the car. While the engine is running, turn on the heater to keep body temperature above 90 degrees, warding off hypothermia and frostbite.

7 | **Remain active.**
While sitting in the car, periodically rotate your torso from side to side and move your arms and legs to keep blood flow moving.

8 | **Huddle for warmth.**
If traveling with others, sit in a row in the back seat, wrapping your arms and legs together to stay warm. Take turns sleeping.

9 **Forage.**
If the snow stops, walk 50 yards along the shoulder in either direction of your car in search of water, cast-off fast food containers, edible plants, or road kill. Never let your vehicle out of sight.

10 **Eat snow.**
Keep hydrated by eating chunks of the cleanest snow you can find.

11 **Build a tire signal fire.**
Remove the spare tire from the trunk, or remove one tire from the wheel of the car using a tire jack. Set the tire on the roadway or on the ground near the road cleared of snow. Fill up the center of the tire with dry sticks and paper products from your car and ignite it with the car's cigarette lighter or any other means of ignition. Keep the fire burning with paper products until the fire achieves the 400 degrees necessary to ignite the tire itself. Once lit, a tire

will produce a thick black smoke. Do not inhale the smoke, as it contains carbon monoxide, sulfur dioxide, and numerous other toxic chemicals.

Be Aware

- Symptoms of carbon monoxide poisoning include chest tightness, fatigue, dizziness, vomiting, and muscle weakness.
- If afflicted with hypothermia or frostbite, do not drink caffeine or alcohol. Caffeine will amplify the negative effects of cold on the body, while alcohol can slow the heart and restrict blood flow.
- Before setting out in winter conditions, stock your trunk with snow chains, bottled water, food, blankets, and signal flares.
- Only burn your tires if you have exhausted every effort to restart your vehicle, and no vehicles have come by in 48 hours.

JUNK IN THE TRUNK:
MUST-HAVE EMERGENCY ITEMS

- Local map, atlas, or GPS system
- Crank or battery-powered radio and batteries
- Large flashlight and batteries
- Matches or lighter
- Basic automotive tool kit
- First-aid kit
- Emergency flares
- Spare tire
- Jack
- Jumper cables
- 3 days worth of nonperishable food
- 6 quarts of water per adult passenger
- Duct tape
- Pepper spray, emergency whistle
- Collapsible shovel
- Ice scraper, rock salt (for cold weather)
- Insulated sleeping bag
- 2 two-by-fours
- Rain poncho and boots
- License and registration
- Phone charger
- Emergency roadside assistance phone number
- Bribe Money

HOW TO BRACE FOR IMPACT

1 **Stay in control until the last possible moment.**
Keep your hands on the wheel and continue efforts to steer and avoid the obstacle until all options are exhausted.

2 **Perform a seatbelt check.**
Tug quickly on the lap and shoulder of your belt to make sure you are clicked in and the belt is fully tightened.

3 **Lean back.**
Move your body fully back in your seat and lay your head against the head rest.

4 **Release the wheel.**
Take your hands off of the steering wheel. At the moment of impact, the wheel may jerk violently, transmitting the shock to

Hold onto your seatbelt and lift your feet off the pedals.

your body and breaking your fingers
and thumbs.

5 | **Hang onto your seatbelt.**
Clutch the seatbelt with both hands near
the place where the lap belt clicks into the
shoulder belt, so both hands are secure and
out of the way of the deploying front and
side airbags.

6 | **Lift your feet off the pedals.**
Remove your feet from both the brake and
accelerator pedals to avoid having your
ankles and shins crushed on impact.

7 | **Close your eyes.**
Protect your vision by closing your eyes
tightly. Most cars have shatter-resistant
glass, but it may not hold together in
certain impacts.

MOST COMMON FATAL CRASHES

Type of Crash	Percent of Overall Accidents	Percent of Fatal Accidents
Rear Impact	30%	5%
Side Impact	29%	20%
Stationary Object	16%	32%
Animal	5%	4%
Rollover	2%	11%
Head-On	2%	10%
Cyclist or Pedestrian	2%	14%

HOW TO PEE IN THE CAR WHILE STUCK IN TRAFFIC

1 **Cover the seat.**
Arching your back to elevate your butt from the seat, completely cover the front seat of the car with paper towels or newspaper.

2 **Find a container.**
Look around the interior of the car for a cup with an open or resealable top, such as a travel mug, to-go cup, or refillable sports bottle. Widen the top of a plastic water bottle with a pocket knife or scissors. Avoid containers with small openings, such as glass bottles or aluminum cans.

3 **Empty the container.**
Roll down the window and dump the contents of the container outside of the car,

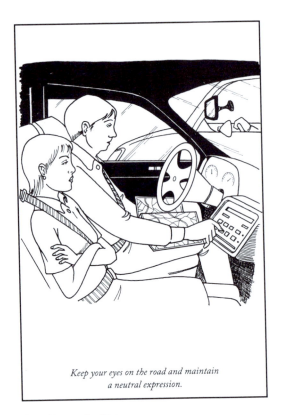

Keep your eyes on the road and maintain
a neutral expression.

careful not to splash adjacent vehicles or passersby, or damage the paint on your car.

4 Pull down your pants.
Keeping one hand on the wheel, reach down with your other hand, unbutton, unfasten, or adjust your clothing just enough to expose your nether regions.

5 Cradle the container between your legs.
Angle the opening of the container forward at a 45 degree angle.

6 Aim into the top of the container.
Cover your private parts, and the container, with a sweater or roadmap.

7 Do your business.
While you are urinating, keep your eyes fixed on the road and maintain a neutral facial expression. If you have passengers, turn up the radio to hide the noise of the stream.

8 **Readjust your clothing.**
Set the container in the car's cup-holder
and refasten and readjust your clothing
as normal.

9 **Dump out the contents of the container**
Roll down the window and dump the
contents of the container outside of the
car, being careful not to splash adjacent
vehicles or passersby, or damage the paint
on your car.

Be Aware
Holding in your urine for extended periods
can put you at risk for urinary tract infections,
and can distend your bladder, leading to an
increased urinary frequency in the future.

INSTANT SOLUTION

IMPROVISE A SUNSHADE

Unroll the driver's side window ½ inch. Remove your jacket, shirt, or blouse. Tuck it evenly across the top of the window, then close the window to hold the garment in place to block harsh sunlight. Lift the garment for visibility when changing lanes in that direction.

HOW TO PARALLEL PARK A TRACTOR TRAILER

1 **Pull ahead of the space you want.**
Find a parking space that is one and a half times the length of your truck. (If your truck is 20 feet long, your space should be 30 feet long). Pull up ahead of the space, leaving at least two arm lengths of space between you and the car or truck next to you.

2 **Turn on your emergency lights.**

3 **Back up.**
As you put the truck in reverse, give three short horn blasts to alert anyone on the street behind you.

4 **Stop.**
When, in your curb-side mirror, you see the front end of your truck's trailer even with the rear bumper of the car or truck in front of your chosen space, brake and put the truck back in drive.

5 **Turn the wheel.**
Turn the wheel of the tractor away from the curb as far as possible.

6 **Swing out.**
Check for oncoming traffic, and then apply gas, swinging the tractor out into the roadway as you back the trailer into the spot. (The trailer will move in the opposite direction that you are turning the wheel).

7 **Cut back.**
When the back curbside wheel of the trailer hits the curb, stop, turn the wheel all the way in the other direction, and pull forward.

Tricky Situations

Swing the tractor out into the roadway as you back the trailer into the spot.

8 | **Repeat steps 6 and 7.**
Check both side-mirrors to gauge the position of the trailer. If the mirror's blind spot keeps you from seeing the exact position of the trailer, get out of the truck, walk around, and look. Repeat steps 6 and 7 until the trailer is well into the spot and the tractor is not jutting out into the road. Trailers are not designed to go efficiently in reverse and may need dozens of small adjustments to be navigated properly into the space.

9 | **Double check your curb distance and ramp room.**
Maneuver the tractor until it is no further than 18 inches from the curb, and the back end is at least 18 feet from the car or truck behind it, so the ramp can come down and moving trolleys can get in and out. If your distances are insufficient, pull out from the space and start again.

Be Aware

- The narrower the street, the less room you will have to swing out your tractor in step 5. If you are parking on a two or three lane street, without minimal oncoming traffic, leave more space between your truck and the car next to you, and swing out further.
- Before attempting to navigate city streets in a moving truck, know the height of your vehicle. When approaching overhanging tree branches, ease forward very slowly to avoid damage to the truck or tree. Do not drive under low-hanging power lines.
- Many municipalities require you to give advance notice to the police department to park a moving truck or other tractor-trailer for even a short period of time.

INSTANT SOLUTION

GET A CAR OUT OF SAND

*Place floormats (or wood, if available) under the front tires.
Accelerate slowly until tires gain traction, and maintain
slow, even speed until the car returns to the roadway.*

HOW TO DRIVE IN A HURRICANE

⭐ Roll up the windows.

⭐ Turn on your high beams.

⭐ Do not drive next to or behind buses and trucks.
A strong gust of wind can topple a large vehicle over onto your car. Slow down to allow heavy vehicles such as buses and trucks to get ahead and past you. Do not drive behind buses and trucks, as their tires will kick up large amounts of water from the roadway and send it back into your windshield.

⭐ Weigh down the car.
Fill the trunk of your car with heavy objects such as bricks, lumber, appliances, or debris

*Avoid driving behind buses and trucks as their tires
will kick up large amounts of water.*

for ballast, to keep the wind from grabbing and flinging the car.

★ **Reduce your speed.**
Drive at 10 miles per hour or less, keeping alert for flying debris and other cars that have stopped or stalled and are blocking the roadway.

★ **Apply the brakes as little as possible.**
In a heavy downpour, there is a significant chance of hydroplaning as water builds up between your wheels and the road. Slow down by taking your foot off the gas rather than applying the brake, and watch for deep puddles.

★ **Note protected and unprotected areas, and adjust your speed accordingly.**
You will be sheltered from the wind when driving in protected areas, such as tunnels. When emerging from the protected area, remember to slow down again.

⭐ **Drive in the middle lane.**
Water will pool more in the outer lanes of the roadway.

⭐ **Be alert for standing water.**
If you cannot see the roadway at the bottom of an area covered by water, do not drive into it. Turn around and find another route. Even if it looks like the water is shallow, there may be hidden pits; water of six inches or higher can cause damage and/or stall your car.

⭐ **Be alert for flash floods.**
Flash floods occur when there is extremely heavy rainfall over a short period of time. They occur most frequently in low-lying areas, such as narrow canyons and valleys. Do not stay in a flooded car; if your car starts to fill up, get out.

Be Aware

Never drive in a tornado. If you are in your car when a tornado approaches, exit your car and lie down on your stomach in a ditch or low-lying area, and cover your face and head with your arms.

How to Drive in a Whiteout

⭐ **Wear sunglasses.**
Don a pair of ultraviolet-blocking sunglasses to prevent snow blindness as the sun reflects off the snow into your eyes.

⭐ **Turn off your lights.**
High-beams, and even regular headlights, can reflect back in severe snow and reduce your visibility. Drive using only your parking lights.

⭐ **Maintain maximum visibility.**
Run the windshield wipers on high to keep the windshield clear; when necessary,

pull over and wipe the windshield clean. Remove condensation from the windows and windshield by turning on the air conditioner to dehumidify the car. Do not use the windshield wiper fluid; if it's low quality, it may freeze on the windshield.

⭐ **Look for visual clues.**
Constantly scan roadway for large objects, such as buildings and telephone poles, that will keep you oriented to the relative position of the horizon line and the roadway.

⭐ **Look for ruts left by other drivers.**
Whenever possible, find the tracks left by other vehicles and drive in them, rather than trying to find your own path down the roadway. This reduces the risk of accident and increases your ability to distinguish the ground apart from the sky.

⭐ **Slow down.**
Drive a maximum of half the posted speed limit and leave at least three car-lengths between you and the driver ahead.

⭐ **Do not pass other cars.**
Stay in your lane. Use the running lights of cars ahead of you to help guide your way, traveling in the ruts left by their wheels.

⭐ **Brake steadily.**
Apply your brakes only when absolutely necessary. Avoid tapping or slamming down on the brakes.

⭐ **Avoid rivulets.**
Watch for small patches of water or melted or semifrozen ice running across the roadway. Steer around such patches when possible. If you must drive over them, do so even more slowly.

⭐ **Under-react.**

If you hit a slick of ice or snow, or appear to be headed for a collision, do not slam down on the brakes or jerk the steering wheel. React slowly to events, as any ice on the road will exaggerate your car's reaction to events.

Be Aware

When driving in winter, keep your tank half-full at all times to avoid the risk of freezing the gas line.

CHAPTER 2
YOU AND YOUR
FELLOW DRIVERS

@#$&*%!

HOW TO EVADE A PURSUER

Escape Method

1 **Identify the pursuer.**
Note the make, model, color, and any other distinguishing features (including the number of passengers) of the pursuing vehicle to help keep track of it in your escape, especially if it is a common vehicle type.

2 **Drive to a high-traffic environment.**

3 **Drive fast.**
Stay ahead of the flow of traffic.

4 **Weave in and out of lanes.**
Look for gaps between cars and suddenly speed up to shift into the gaps. Do not signal your lane changes.

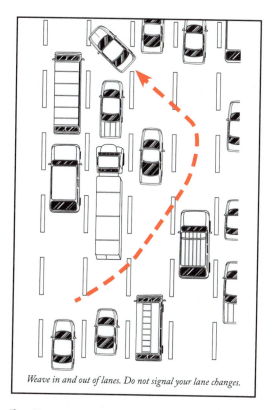

Weave in and out of lanes. Do not signal your lane changes.

5 **Turn frequently and unexpectedly.**
When possible, turn right out of the far
left lane, or right out of the far left lane.

6 **Seek cover near large vehicles.**
Get as many large, eye-line-blocking
vehicles as possible between you and your
pursuer. Ride with one truck or bus in
front of you and another behind, and then
follow the front vehicle into a turn.

7 **Accelerate through yellow lights.**
When you see a traffic light turn yellow,
slow until just before it will turn red, then
accelerate through the intersection at the
last moment. Watch for oncoming traffic.

8 **Pitch your pursuer through a yellow light.**
When you see a traffic light turn yellow,
and your pursuer is slightly behind you
but not in your lane, speed up to the light
as if you intend to speed through it. At
the last second, slam on your brakes and

let your pursuer speed through the light.
Check for oncoming traffic, and then turn.

DISABLING METHOD

1 **Drive normally.**
Do not let on that you know you are being
followed.

2 **Situate your car so that your pursuer is
directly behind you.**
If your pursuer is trying to maintain his
distance, slow down sufficiently so the
traffic between your cars will accelerate
to pass you.

3 **Accelerate gently.**
Once your car is directly in front of your
pursuer, accelerate gently to put 20 or 30 feet
of road between your vehicles.

4 **Slam on the brakes and throw the car
in reverse.**

5 **Accelerate backwards into your pursuer's car.**
Striking your pursuer's front bumper going at least 15 miles per hour will cause his airbag to deploy, locking the starter of his vehicle.

6 **Put the car in drive and accelerate forward.**
Drive away quickly.

CAN I HAVE YOUR RIDE?

Most Popular Cars with Thieves

1. Honda Civic
2. Honda Accord
3. Toyota Camry
4. Ford F-Series Pickup
5. Dodge Ram
6. Chevrolet C/K 1500 Pickup
7. Nissan Sentra
8. Dodge Caravan
9. Saturn SL
10. Acura Integra

Most Popular Cars with Consumers

1. Ford F-Series Pickup
2. Chevy Silverado
3. Toyota Camry
4. Honda Accord
5. Toyota Corolla
6. Honda Civic
7. Nissan Altima
8. Chevy Impala
9. Dodge Ram
10. Honda CR-V

BAD DRIVING BEHAVIOR

Acceptable	Questionable	Unacceptable
Applying lipstick	Applying eyeliner	Giving self pedicure
Talking to passengers	Talking on cell phone	Writing and sending e-mail
Checking hair in rearview mirror	Combing hair	Shaving
Drinking to-go beverage	Eating drive-through meal	Making a sandwich
Adjusting tie	Tying tie	Changing shirt

HOW TO TELL IF YOUR CAR HAS BEEN TAMPERED WITH

1 **Examine the ground around your car.**
Get down on all fours and crawl along the
ground around your car up to a distance
of 25 feet away, looking for small bits of
wire or wire insulation, discarded scraps
of tape, or puttylike lumps.

2 **Examine the locks and windows.**
Run a flashlight along the cracks between
the doors and the doorframes, looking for
small wires. Using a magnifying glass,
examine the door locks and windows,
and the area directly surrounding them,
for scrapes or scratches indicating forced
entry. Check the seam around the trunk;
open the trunk and make sure the mats

have not been moved, and there are no unfamiliar objects or bits of wire or wire insulation.

3 **Examine the gas tank.**
Run your hands over the crack between the gas tank cover to make sure it's flush and shows no signs of prying. Use a magnifying glass to look for scuff marks or scratches. Open the gas tank cover and sniff the tank for strong, nongas odors.

4 **Open the hood.**
Shine your flashlight around the engine block, particularly the wiring, to see if anything is disconnected or if there are any new wires present. Run the light along the firewall (the back wall of the engine, separating the fuel tank from the passenger compartment) to make sure it has not been sabotaged.

5 | **Use a mirror to examine the underside of the car.**
Slide a small handheld mirror under the chassis and slowly move it clockwise around the underside of the car, examining the reflected image for foreign objects attached to the vehicle.

6 | **Check your brakes.**
Lie down a foot away from the front of the car and sweep your flashlight underneath it, looking for a puddle of greasy liquid, which may be brake fluid that has been drained from your vehicle. Run one finger slowly along the brake lines, from each brake pad back to the master cylinder, feeling for pinholes or cuts.

7 | **Look into the exhaust pipe.**
Shine a flashlight into the pipe to look for foreign objects.

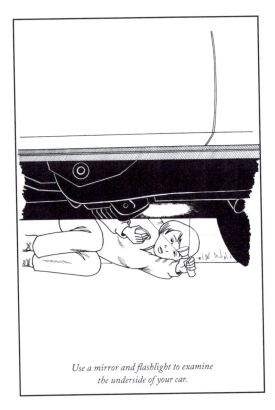

*Use a mirror and flashlight to examine
the underside of your car.*

8 | **Inspect your wheels and tires.**
Run your hands all the way around each tire to feel for minor punctures or small slashes. Feel each lug nut to make sure it is still properly tightened. Check the air pressure of each tire with a tire pressure gauge to make sure no one has let the air out of your tires.

9 | **Examine the front seats for signs of intrusion.**
Before opening the car door, look through the window for signs that someone has been in the car. Note whether the angle of the seats has been altered, if the rearview mirror has been redirected, or if the floor mats have been moved or disturbed.

10 | **Take a deep breath.**
Once settled in the driver's seat, sniff the air. The odor of gasoline within the vehicle can indicate that the gas tank has been tampered with or punctured.

11 **Look for a planted device.**

Run your fingers along the underside of the passenger and driver's seats in search of foreign objects. Check under the brake and acceleration pedals. Do not apply pressure to the seats until you are satisfied there is nothing beneath them that may be pressure-triggered.

Be Aware

- The best way to notice any tampering is to know your vehicle well under normal circumstances. Carry a photograph of the inside of your engine so you can check the arrangement of wires against the picture before starting your car each time.
- Always leave objects on your front seat, such as newspapers or tissue boxes, so you can gauge whether someone has moved them when you return to the car.

TOP TEN IN-CAR ACTIVITIES
THAT LEAD TO ACCIDENTS

1. Wireless devices (Cell phones, digital assistants, GPS)

2. In-car communication (Dictating notes-to-self, yelling at children)

3. Internal distractions (Fumbling for dropped phone, looking for items on seat)

4. Grooming (Applying makeup, picking teeth)

5. Dashboard Activities (Finding a radio station, adjusting air conditioning)

6. Eating or drinking

7. External distractions (Rubbernecking, checking out attractive person in oncoming vehicle)

8. Singing or talking to yourself

9. Smoking (Reaching for, lighting, putting out cigarettes)

10. Daydreaming

HOW TO ESCAPE FROM THE TRUNK OF A CAR

1 **Breathe.**
Resist the urge to panic. Trunks are not airtight, which means you will probably die of dehydration or overheating before suffocating, but hyperventilating will deplete the store of oxygen more quickly.

2 **Feel for a safety latch.**
Run your palms slowly and deliberately over every surface of the trunk's interior. The safety latch, if there is one, will most likely be located in the center of the trunk lid. Many car models now come with a safety latch preinstalled; in others, the owner may have installed a store-bought model, typically a white plastic handle dangling on a small piece of cord.

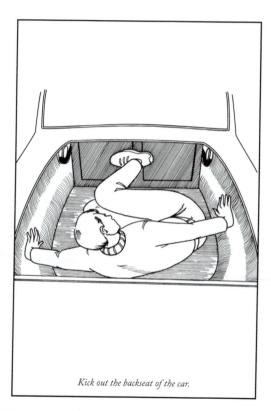

Kick out the backseat of the car.

3 Look for a trunk cable.

Pull up the trunk carpet and search on the driver's side of the car for a cable running from the driver's seat to the trunk. Yank up hard on the cable to pop the trunk.

4 Kick out the backseat of the car.

Brace your back against the rear end of the trunk. Using both legs, kick against the center of the wall separating the trunk from the backseat. Kick once at the center and then once at each of the sides, testing each to see if there is any give. If after three strong kicks you do not feel the wall begin to move, preserve your energy and oxygen and move on to the next step.

5 Search for tools.

Feel carefully around the floor of the trunk for anything long and metal you can use to jimmy the trunk latch, such as a tire iron, pry bar, or long screwdriver. Look under the trunk carpet for any niches or hidden compartments.

6 | **Jimmy the trunk latch.**
Find the trunk latch at the center of the long horizontal crack where the trunk lid meets the base. Jab one end of your sharp metal object at the latch at a 45-degree angle and exert downwards force on the metal object, until you pop the latch and release the trunk.

Be Aware
- The majority of trunk-entrapments occur in a person's own car. Keep a flashlight and crowbar in your car, or install a glow-in-the-dark release mechanism.
- Since 1970, at least 1,250 people have been locked in trunks in the United States, and at least 260 have died.

CHAPTER 3
DRIVING EXTREMES

LOOKS EASIER
IN THE MOVIES

HOW TO SURVIVE A BLOW-OUT ON THE ICE ROAD

1 **Ride with your hand on the door.**
The first sign of a blow-out—a wave of water under the ice that causes a tear in its surface—will be black water seeping through the ice's surface. If black water is visible, move one hand from the steering wheel to the handle of the door.

2 **Speed up.**
Ignore the instinct to brake, which can send the truck into a skid or exacerbate the blow-out by concentrating your weight on the crack. Accelerate by a few miles per hour to carry your weight forward past the crack.

3 **Jump out.**
When the front end of the truck starts to go through the ice, open the door of the cab and leap out.

4 **Roll.**
Upon landing, roll as quickly and as far as possible from the sinking cab.

5 **Stay put.**
Do not wander through the whiteout conditions in search of help, as you can quickly become disoriented. Stay where you are until another vehicle from your convoy can reach you.

AVOID A BLOW-OUT

1 **Go slow.**
Stay below 15 miles per hour to avoid churning up the under-ice waves that lead to blow-outs.

Jump out of the cab as it falls through the ice.

2 Do not stop.
Keep your vehicle moving at all times, as the concentrated heat and weight of a stopped truck can cause the surface of the ice to crack.

3 Know where the other drivers are.
Stay in radio and visual contact with the other members of your convoy to avoid a truck-on-truck collision, which will severely damage the ice floor.

Be Aware

- The ice roads, which can only be driven in the winter when the ice is sufficiently thick, cross the frozen lakes of Canada's Northwest Territories, servicing Canada's diamond mines.
- Until the ice is 42 inches thick, which usually happens in mid-February, the ice road cannot reliably bear the 70-ton weight of a fully loaded truck.

- The ice is most fragile closest to the shoreline.
- The sound of ice cracking beneath your rig is not alarming; frozen sheets of ice are constantly breaking and reforming to adjust to weight. If you don't hear cracking, the ice is too thin.

HERE'S YOUR PROBLEM:
WHEN THINGS WEAR OUT

Oil filters	5,000 to 10,000 miles
Power steering fluid	100,000 miles
Brake fluid	30,000 miles
Brake pads	10,000 to 30,000 miles
Clutch	75,000 to 100,000 miles
Engine	250,000 to 350,000 miles
Taillights	Two to three years
Wiper blades	Six months
Battery	Two years
Exhaust systems/ Mufflers	100,000 miles
Shocks and struts	100,000 to 150,000 miles
Airbags	Ten years
Radiators	Five to six years
Timing belt	60,000 miles to 100,000 miles

HOW TO DRIVE DOWN A FLIGHT OF STAIRS

1   **Aim.**
Set your eyes on a spot dead center over the horizon of the staircase, and steer the car at it.

2   **Floor it.**
When you are twenty feet from the stairs, slam your foot down on the accelerator to get a burst of speed approaching the lip.

3   **Shut your mouth.**
Pull your tongue back in your mouth and grit your teeth to keep them from knocking together as the car bounces down the stairs.

Floor it.

69. *Driving Extremes*

4 **Grip the wheel.**
Hold onto the wheel tightly, and steer to counterbalance each time the car jerks one way or the other as it bounces forward.

5 **Lift your foot from the accelerator.**
As the front bumper crosses the lip of the top stair, lift up your feet. Further acceleration is unnecessary as gravity pulls your vehicle forward, and leaving your feet on the pedals will cause your shins to absorb the shock as the car bangs down the steps.

6 **Floor it again.**
When you feel the back wheel hit the bottom stair, bring your right foot back down on the pedal and give another burst of speed to keep your back bumper from catching on the lip of the bottom step.

7 **Even out.**
Hold tightly to the wheel and steer to regain control of the vehicle.

How to Drive Up a Flight of Stairs

1

Aim and accelerate.
Check both side mirrors to make sure you are giving adequate space on either side. When you are twenty feet from the bottom stair, give a burst of gas.

2

Further accelerate as your front wheel hits the first stair.
Give more gas to take your back wheels up onto the stairs.

3

Maintain speed as you climb.
Continue to accelerate as you go up the stairs, to keep gravity from pulling you back down. Give a final burst of speed as you come over the top.

Be Aware

• If your car is too low to the ground, the underside will be scraped and banged by

the stairs all the way up or down, causing serious damage. Fully inflated tires
will give you more clearance.

- Time permitting, laying down a wooden
ramp across the bottom stair will make
your approach to the uphill drive easier,
and mitigate the effects of low clearance.

- A front-wheel drive car will be more
effective than a rear-wheel drive car,
while an all-wheel drive car is ideal,
since the drive system sends more
traction to the various tires as needed.

Instant Solution

Fire Under the Hood

Pull over and turn off the engine. Do not open the hood.
Exit the car and move at least 100 yards from the vehicle.

HOW TO SURVIVE A ROLLOVER

1 **Pull your feet off the pedals.**
As the car starts to roll, lift your feet from the brake and accelerator pedals and tuck them under the seat to keep your ankles from breaking against the floor of the vehicle.

2 **Let go of the wheel.**
If you are hanging onto the wheel when the car slams into the ground again, the impact will be transmitted through your entire body. Once the car has begun to roll, turning the wheel will not have any effect.

3 **Cross your arms over your chest.**
Keep your arms and hands as far as possible from the windows of the car as the window side slams into the ground.

4 | **Brace yourself with your feet.**
Once the car is upside down, find purchase somewhere with both feet, either on the windshield, the driver's side window, or on the ceiling of the car.

5 | **Count to sixty.**
Remain still and suspended from your seatbelt until you are certain that your vehicle has stopped moving, and that any other vehicles involved in the accident have stopped moving and are not sliding across the roadway into yours.

6 | **Check yourself for injuries.**
While hanging onto the seatbelt with one hand, pat your body with the other hand to check for injuries. Run your hand through your hair and over scalp. In case of any injury, do not move.

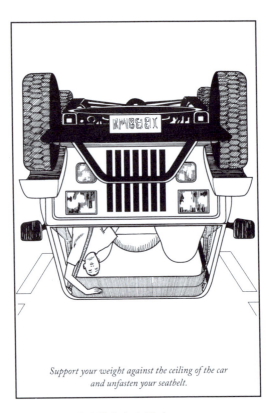

Support your weight against the ceiling of the car and unfasten your seatbelt.

7 **If you appear to be uninjured, reach up and stabilize yourself.**
As you are dangling from the seatbelt, slowly bring one hand up and lay it firmly against the ceiling of the car.

8 **Unfasten your seatbelt.**
When you are certain your weight is fully supported by your hands and feet, un-click your seatbelt and drop down onto the ceiling.

9 **Get out of the car.**
Check for oncoming traffic. Open the door and exit the vehicle. Get clear of the roadway and await emergency personnel.

Be Aware

- Rollovers occur when a driver loses control of the vehicle, it slides sideways, and hits a "trip," such as a curb or guardrail. A second common cause is a driver taking a turn or curve too quickly.

- Rollovers account for only three percent of total accidents, but cause about a quarter of fatal crashes. More than half the people killed in single-vehicle crashes die in rollovers.
- Many rollover injuries occur after the accident itself, when the victim unbuckles her seatbelt and falls to the roof of the car.
- Rollovers are more common in pickup trucks than cars—mostly in SUVs, defined as passenger vehicles with high ground clearance (generally eight inches or higher) and with the same platform as a truck.
- Always wear your seatbelt.

THOSE WERE THE DAYS:
THE MODEL T VS. AVERAGE CAR TODAY

	The Original Model T	Modern 4-Door Sedan
Price	$850	$28,400
Manufacturing Time	1 car every 93 minutes	50 to 60 cars every hour
Cars Sold	10,000 (first year)	16 million annually
Horsepower	20	160
Top Speed	45 mph	142 mph
Weight	1,200 lbs	3,577 lbs
Price of a Gallon of Gas	7 to 10 cents	$2 to $3
Miles per Gallon	25	21

HOW TO BAIL OUT OF A CAR AT HIGH SPEEDS

1 **Look for the best place to bail out.**
Try to bail out into a body of water or into foliage. Failing that, drive as close to the curbside as possible to avoid leaping into traffic.

2 **Unbuckle your seatbelt.**
Steer the car with one hand as you unbuckle the seatbelt with the other. Bring the lap and chest belts fully clear of your body to avoid entanglement.

3 **Tuck your chin.**
Close your mouth tightly and angle your neck down until your chin rests on your breastbone.

Hold your arms across your chest.

4 **Brace your feet.**
Remove both feet from the pedals and place them squarely on the floorboards of the vehicle, in front of the pedals.

5 **Open the door.**
In one swift movement, grasp the door handle and fling open the door of the vehicle.

6 **Spring out of the car.**
As soon as the door is completely open, push against the floor of the car with both feet to throw your body upward and outward from the car.

7 **Cross your arms.**
With each hand, grab the opposite shoulder tightly, keeping your arms across your chest.

8 **Land and roll.**
As you hit the ground, roll as far from the car as possible, to avoid your rear wheels and other cars.

DAILY COMMUTE TIMES

Mexico City, Mexico	4 hours
Bangkok, Thailand	4 hours
São Paolo, Brazil	2 hours 30 minutes
Dubai, United Arab Emirates	1 hour 45 minutes
Cairo, Egypt	1 hour 33 minutes
Mumbai, India	1 hour 30 minutes
London, England	1 hour 26 minutes
Toronto, Canada	1 hour 19 minutes
Beijing, China	1 hour 10 minutes
New York City, United States	1 hour 9 minutes

HOW TO STOP A CAR WITH MAL-FUNCTIONING BRAKES

1 **Keep your eyes on the road.**
Until you are able to stop, your most urgent priority is to continue to steer the car.

2 **Pump brakes.**
Build pressure with remaining brake fluid by pumping the brakes continuously.

3 **Downshift.**
If you are in a manual transmission car, engage the clutch and downshift; do so again and then again until you are in your transmission's lowest gear. In an automatic transmission, move the gear shifter to the lowest gear, from Drive down to Second and then into First.

*Drive alongside a wall or building
to slow your vehicle's speed.*

4 **Engage the emergency brake.**
Depending on the make and model of your vehicle, the emergency brake may be a hand lever located between the driver and the front passenger, or a foot-operated pedal to the left of the regular driving pedals, close to the driver's side door of the vehicle. Pull on the emergency brake gently in a steady, constant motion.

5 **Drive up a hill.**
If driving on the highway, look for exit ramp that will take you up hill; in the city, turn off the road onto an uphill street. Gravity will slow down your vehicle as you go up the hill.

6 **Seek a soft landing.**
Steer the car off the road into an environment that will do the minimum amount of damage to the car and passengers, such as a patch of bushes, or a snowy field.

7 | **Scrub off speed.**
Drive alongside a wall, guard rail, or the side of a building. Bring the car closer and closer until the side of the car is "kissing" the wall or rail, sending off sparks and slowing down the rate of speed with a series of small collisions.

8 | **Turn off the engine.**
As a last resort, turn the car off. The rate of acceleration will rapidly decrease; however, steering becomes impossible.

I TAKE THAT BACK

Year	Nature of problem
1971	Engine mounts fell off
1971	Seatbelt decay
1972	Windshield wipers flew off in storms
1973	Steering assembly disabled by stones from roadway
1978	Gas tank subject to explosion
1981	Suspension bolts came loose, impeding steering
1987	Engine compartment fires
1996	Steering column fires
1996	Ignition systems catch fire
2004	Defective tailgate cables
2005	Faulty headlights
2007	Cruise control switch bursts into flames

MAJOR SAFETY RECALLS

Model(s)	Number of cars affected
GMs including Camaro, Chevrolet, G Series, Impala, P Series, C Series and Townsmen	6.7 million
Fords including Ranchero, Lincoln, and Mercury	4.1 million
VW Bugs	3.7 million
GMs including LeSabre, Caprice, and Impala	3.7 million
Ford Pinto	1.5 million
GMs including Century and Malibu	5.8 million
Ford almost all models	3.6 million
Ford various models	8 million
Fords including Escort, Mustang, Thunderbird, and Lincoln Town Car	8.6 million
GMs including Silverado, Sierra, Escalades and Avalanche	3.6 million
Toyota Corollas and others	1.4 million
Fords, including Lincoln and Mercury	3.6 million

INDEX

ACKNOWLEDGMENTS

David Borgenicht would like to thank Sarah O'Brien, Steve Mockus, Jenny Kraemer, Brenda Brown, and Ben Winters for making this book happen. He promises each of you a free oil and filter change at 5,000 miles.

Ben H. Winters would like to thank the following automotive experts: Mark Cox at Bridgestone Winter Driving School, Robert Prevost at RacingSchools.com, Mike Burke of Driver's East, trucker A.J. Jones, and the good and safe people at the Insurance Institute of Highway Safety and AAA.

ABOUT THE AUTHORS

David Borgenicht is the creator and coauthor of all the books in the *Worst-Case Scenario* series, and is president and publisher of Quirk Books (www.irreference.com). His own worst-case car scenario took place when he nearly drove into a ditch at night in Virginia Beach, Virginia. He lives in Philadelphia.

Ben H. Winters writes *Worst-Case Scenario* books and some other silly stuff you can read about at www.Ben-HWinters.com. While parking his car in his Brooklyn neighborhood, he very rarely has to drive down any stairs.

Brenda Brown is an illustrator and cartoonist whose work has been published in many books and publications, including the *Worst-Case Scenario* series, *Esquire, Reader's Digest, USA Weekend, 21st Century Science & Technology,* the *Saturday Evening Post,* and the *National Enquirer.* Her Web site is www.webtoon.com.

MORE WORST-CASE SCENARIO PRODUCTS

VISIT THESE WEBSITES FOR MORE WORST-CASE SCENARIO PRODUCTS:

- ✪ Board games
  www.universitygames.com
- ✪ Gadgets
  www.protocoldesign.com
- ✪ Mobile
  www.namcogames.com
- ✪ Posters and puzzles
  www.aquariusimages.com/wcs.html

For updates, new scenarios, and more, visit:
www.worstcasescenarios.com

To order books visit:
www.chroniclebooks.com/worstcase

MORE WORST-CASE SCENARIOS

HANDBOOKS

- The Worst-Case Scenario Survival Handbook
- Travel
- Dating & Sex
- Golf
- Holidays
- Work
- College
- Weddings
- Parenting
- Extreme Edition
- Life

ALMANACS

- History
- Great Outdoors
- Politics

CALENDARS

- Daily Survival Calendar
- Daily Survival Calendar: Golf

POCKET GUIDES

- Dogs
- Breakups
- Retirement
- New York City
- Cats
- Meetings
- San Francisco
- Cars